Reinventing Your Style

Reinventing Your Style

7 Strategies for Looking
Dynamic,
Powerful,
and Inspiring

by Jennifer Butler

Reinventing Your Style
Los Angeles, California

ISBN 978-1-60530-680-3

Butler, Jennifer:
    Reinventing Your Style by Jennifer Butler

Photo Credits
Photography by Maria Rangel of Mariaphotography.com as noted:
Back cover photo of Jennifer Butler also featured on page 12;
photos of models on pages 25, 36, 48, 55, 56, 57, 59, 65, 76, 77, 78,
79, 83, 84, 85, 87, 93, 94, 95, 96
All other photography by istockphoto.com

Book design and illustrations by Hortensia Chu
Pre-press production by McMac Publications
Printed by Pace Lithographers Inc., City of Industry, California

Printed in the United States of America
FIRST EDITION

05 04 03 02 01
5 4 3 2 1

Part of the proceeds from the sale of this book goes to the Agape
Community for the growth of spiritual living on the planet.

Contents

*Dedicated to Suzanne Caygill, founder of the seasonal essence
and color work over 65 years ago.*

*To Sid Syvertson, whom I consider to be a masterful entrepreneur,
who taught me to share my gift with the world.
To Diana Syvertson, who is my friend, my sister, and spiritual partner,
who has inspired the growth and development of my work
and who truly lives it herself.*

*To all my clients who have had the courage and vulnerability
to reveal their authentic selves
through the colors and clothes they wear.*

Emanation of Light (Autumn)

The full majesty of Mother Nature is reflected in
her complexity and abundance.

To be ideally attired, impeccably clad, one needs to have a life-long fashion expert foresee the best that clothes can bring out in us. Jennifer Butler is THE ONE. She clearly reads one's skin tone, eye color, hair nuances, and then discovers and decides how to make you the most attractive, active, and positively attention-getting sartorial splendor anywhere.

Jennifer invested time to look at me deeply, came to understand what would bring out my radiance, charisma and beauty and then, proceeded to edit out all the many clothes on my shelves and in my closet that did not, would not and could not work for or with me. She has proven to me that being impeccably dressed for success and to impress, requires someone that has distinctions of textures, weaves, seasons and color possibilities that most of us will never have.

All the greats always have mentors that coach them. We each need a Jennifer to mentor us, to perfect our fashion, style and attire, so we look our best to present ourselves attractively to the world. Everyone sees us externally first and instantly judges us, before they really get to know who we really are. Jennifer is a mensch. She knows how to perfect one's fashionable attire, make you feel and look great and get phenomenal results. What she does works every time. Read her great book and you too can come to master the fine art of dressing for success and to memorably impress.

Mark Victor Hansen
Co-creator, #1 *New York Times* best-selling series *Chicken Soup for the Soul*
Co-author, *Cracking the Millionaire Code* and *The One Minute Millionaire*

Have you ever had the experience of standing in front of a mirror at a department store, looking at the outfit you have just tried on, and know that something isn't quite right but can't put your finger on it? Have you ever tried on a blouse or shirt and noticed that one can look really great and another matronly? Or that some people can wear a mixture of patterns, prints, and tons of jewelry and look fabulous, while others get lost in their outfits?

I'm Jennifer Butler and when I started in the fashion industry over 25 years ago, I experienced all this and so much more. In all my training, there didn't seem to be any fundamental rules to follow that made any sense. If something didn't look right, you just found a skinnier mannequin or model to put it on. I wanted to be able to discern the technical reasons why something worked on one person and not on another. So, by using my background in art history, fashion, and sociology, I created the seven principles of design.

.. the context of these principles is to be in the affirmative.

These principles are based on my observations of Mother Nature and great works of art. If you look at Mother Nature, there is a natural rhythm, harmony, and symmetry that is beautiful every time, whether observing an animal or a beautiful landscape. I noticed this same rhythm in great works of art. So, I decided to take a closer look at what I was experiencing visually and I began dressing that way. After all, each of us is our own great work of art and creation of Mother Nature. What I discovered is that when studying Mother Nature and art, there was a pattern and repetition that I was able to discern. By following these principles, I was able to create a template for myself on how to hit a homerun with my clothing choices every time. No more mistakes hanging in my closet with the tags still on. The context of these principles is to be in the affirmative.

You are always congruent and you always look beautiful.

Oftentimes when we look at ourselves in an outfit we might say, well, if I were just thinner, younger, in better shape, or better looking the outfit would work.

What I'm offering is that you are always congruent and you always look beautiful. If something doesn't look right, it's the outfit that doesn't really live up to your beauty, not the other way around. You are perfect in every way, and I will give you the vocabulary and the observation so you can interpret yourself that way. These design principles not only apply to the way you dress, but to many aspects of your life including decorating your home. My desire is for you to discover your natural beauty and learn how to use design to eliminate buying things you don't wear, create a wardrobe that works, and buy clothing that flatters your personal body design.

The design principles that I will be addressing in this book are: first, the principle of contrast, then texture, complexity, scale and proportion, geometry, visual weight, and last, print selection.

I wish I could tell you that I was a child prodigy like Mozart and all the great information in this book just flowed through me. But this was not the case. Learning to develop my own personal style has been a struggle and a challenge… a struggle because I kept looking outside myself for the answers and a challenge because I did not appreciate or recognize my own beauty.

My world changed when my mother decided to open a fabric store called the Calico Cat in Hibbing, Minnesota in order to raise the funds for her six children to go to college (I have 5 brothers). I had a heyday of designing window displays, and making clothes made for myself or by a seamstress. Since I was a slave to fashion magazines and Vogue Patterns, I wore every color and style imaginable. My collection of clothes was so unusual that, while at college I became the "unofficial" stylist for everyone's date weekend. This recognition allowed me to be rated "Best Dressed" and after three years of representing my school, I won the Glamour Top Ten College girls in 1969.

Glamour invited us to New York City and I was introduced to retail heaven. Bloomingdale's accepted me into their executive training program. In order to be "fashionable," I began buying a collection of clothes "on sale" with the justification of having to look good all the time. When my mortgage began competing with my

I invite you to come and observe beauty with me – your beauty.

Four years ago, I chose to go "platinum gray". Let me add a new colloquialism, "Gray haired women do have more fun." On the path to my own authenticity, this choice has been a crucial step.

clothing budget something needed to change. My role models at the time were Diana Ross, Twiggy, and Marisa Berenson. I just knew that if I kept looking like them my life would turn out successfully.

After Bloomingdale's, I was hired by Vogue Patterns. I worked in the department that created all the fashion shows that traveled throughout the U.S. This is when I had an "aha" moment. I had styled a beautiful party dress in an imported cotton ottoman with intricate seams and details. The instructions read: "Have a brunette wear the outfit."

Simple enough, but when the model in Phoenix looked fabulous, and her so-called look-a-like in Dallas did not, I knew something was up. I started asking myself the question, "How does someone develop their own personal style? What are the ingredients to looking like oneself and loving it?" With this question, my life changed again!

I entered the personal growth movement. Image gave way to authenticity. I moved from New York City to San Francisco and Los Angeles. In the early 80's, I had the privilege of studying with Suzanne Caygill, the originator of the process called Color Analysis. We spent hours painting and referencing great works of art. After hours and hours of observation, I started to notice patterns and rhythms emerge. In a painting of a spring landscape, for example, the blue of the sky was in the blue of the birds and flowers. The shape of the tree mirrored the shape of a building and the shape of a person. The answers were right before my eyes all the time, waiting for me to see. It's simple really. The answer lies in repetition. However, the challenge lies in our ability to really see ourselves. I invite you to come and observe beauty with me – your beauty. By arming you with a vocabulary and a new level of self observation, against Mother Nature's backdrop, you will develop the tools to become your own work of art.

By focusing on our assets, we know that everything we have is already within. As Mother Nature frames us as her great work of art, we become educated in creating a harmonious, balanced, and integrated appearance to become powerfully connected to all around us.

As you move through the pages you will notice first an image of Mother Nature, then an animal or art object, then a reference to a person. See how they relate to themselves and then to you. Start to notice your own design pattern and how it can emerge through your clothing choices and accessories.

In my life, getting dressed is a spiritual experience because I believe that my presentation is an extension of my soul. Here are 10 principles I live by. I invite you to integrate these positive affirmations into your life, as well.

POSITIVE AFFIRMATIONS

I am a unique expression of God's creation on this planet.

When I let go of my negative illusions about myself, I am free to embrace my natural self.

I am an extension of Mother Nature and therefore an integral part of the universe.

I am perfect just the way I am. I don't need to change myself in any way.

Authentic radiant beauty lies within me and cannot be defined by someone or something.

My clothes can be an extension of my inner self and inner radiance.

I can dress myself in a way that is inspiring to others.

I can wear colors that enliven me and therefore enliven the planet.

I can be a walking celebration everyday just by the colors and clothes I wear.

When my outer expression is also an inner expression of myself, I show up powerfully, beautifully and authentically.

ONE

CONTRAST

THE PRINCIPLE OF CONTRAST

The first principle is contrast. This is a measure of the balance between the coloring of your hair, skin, and eyes. Specifically, we are comparing the difference between light and dark. We want to reflect the same level of light versus dark into the level of contrast in the clothes you wear. The highest level of contrast would be black and white and the lowest level of contrast would be subtle shades of one color. When you wear your native level of contrast, you make yourself fully visible for someone else because your clothes are repeating, not competing with your native coloring, giving an overall picture of balance and symmetry to the viewer.

When you wear too strong a contrast, your coloring is overpowered and people see your clothes, they don't see you. How many times have you been complimented by someone saying they liked your outfit or the color of your dress rather than complimenting you? The outfit has a louder voice than you do. By comparison, when you wear too low of a contrast, your head and your voice overpowers your clothes, and your body disappears along with your message. With communication being over 55% visual, we can't afford to not be seen. This incongruency waters down the impact of your message and you will have to work much harder to get your point across. I like to think of this as being no different than listening to the radio and suddenly the signal gets weak and I'm straining to hear over the static. It's equally as annoying when you are dressed in a way that is in opposition to your energy or your message. As a result, what most people do is to subconsciously tune out.

Let's review contrast in terms of Mother Nature first where we have a common understanding. High contrast appears in many forms in the animal kingdom as in a zebra, a toucan with his vivid yellow beak, a panda bear, or a black jaguar. I know that a jaguar is all one color and I will explain later why he is considered high contrast. Medium contrast appears in spotted leopards, giraffes, peacocks, and racoons. While low contrast appears in elephants, brown bears, camels, rattlesnakes, and Siamese cats.

Let's see if you can find your level of contrast. Get in front of a mirror, and first look at the contrast between your hair and skin. Is your hair light (blonde, champagne or mushroom), medium (light brown, pecan, strawberry blonde, amber) or dark (auburn, mahogany, black)? Next, how about your skin? Light skin would be alabaster, cameo or porcelain skin. Medium skin would be tawny peach, light bronze, tan, light olive, cafe latte, or medium rose. Dark skin would be red bronze, rose bronze, rose copper, Indian red, deep olive or deep amber. Next, look at your eyes versus your skin. Are your eyes light (baby blue, light hazel, light bronze, seafoam green), medium (blue, nutmeg, maple brown, pine needle green, or hazel) or dark (cinnamon or copper brown, onyx, black-brown, or walnut)? Finally, take a look at your eyes in relation to your hair. Again we are comparing the relationship of lightness and darkness to each other. If at least two categories don't match then focus on the primary contrast which is between your hair and skin.

Here we have some examples of contrast. You could have dark hair and light skin and dark or medium eyes, like Jackie Onassis. This would make you a high contrast person. This means you can handle the highest level of contrast which is black and white or navy and pink or dark brown and ivory. If you have medium brown hair, medium light skin and medium dark eyes, like Jennifer Anniston or Vanessa Williams, you are medium contrast. Your level of contrast would be equivalent to the values of brown mixed with camel, for example, or brown and orange. Finally, low contrast has an overall very blended look, which means your hair, skin and eyes are softly blended like blond hair, light blue eyes and light skin – examples would be Melanie Griffith or Meryl Streep. Low contrast would be equivalent to the values of ivory and peach or black and brown.

Now, remember the black jaguar I referenced earlier as high contrast even though he is all one color? For people of darker skin like African Americans or East Indians or like the jaguar, the coloring between their hair, skin and eyes is all in the same deep or dark value. In those cases we look at the contrast of the hair, skin, and eyes and compare that to the whites of the eyes and teeth. It's important to note that teeth and eyes can range from bright white to warm yellow to soft gray. Bright white being high contrast, and soft bone to soft gray being medium contrast. Low contrast would be deeper gray or beige.

Hopefully after reading about the different levels of contrast, you've been able to identify yours. This doesn't mean that you can never stray from your native level of contrast in your clothing choices, but now that you are aware of your level, there are two guidelines I'd like to share with you if you are going to wear a contrast level that is lower or higher than your native level of contrast. If you're going to wear something that's lower contrast than you are, be sure to wear a lot of texture, design, or accessories to enliven your overall presentation because native contrast has a dynamic that requires more strength than low contrast alone can provide. If you are going to wear a higher contrast than is native to your coloring, try to wear your hair color on the bottom half. Whenever you wear your hair color, whether that be champagne or pecan, taupe or brown, and you combine that with a dark color like navy or black, your hair color will bring balance to your presentation so that your clothes don't speak louder than you.

Contrast
The difference in value between light to dark.

1 Notice the soft subtle blending of her coloring.

2 The camel is tone on tone of one color.

3 Notice the colors are more blended with each other.

MEDIUM CONTRAST equals brown and camel

1 Notice the brown spots in relation to the light sand skin.

2 Notice the medium dark brown hair and eyes in contrast to her skin.

3 Notice the rich brown tones contrasting with the lighter hues of terracotta.

1 Notice the high contrast of the black versus white in the stripes.

2 Notice the deep rich skin contrasting with the whites of the eyes.

3 Notice the contrast of the white snow against the darkness of the trees.

CONTRAST WITH JAGUAR

1 Notice the strong contrast of the dark rich coat of fur and the strong color of its eyes.

2 The children have a more blended lighter skin tone, almost blending with their lips. They have medium light brows and dark irises with soft white for the eyes and teeth. We would give the children a range from low to medium contrast. They can wear blended tones and some medium tones like camel and brown.

3 Notice that her hair, skin, brows and irises are all about the same medium dark tone. If we look at the whites of her eyes and teeth they are in the medium range, a warm beige as compared to stark white. She, therefore, is in the medium contrast range and can wear camel and brown.

4 The key to contrast in dark-skinned people is the whites of the eyes and teeth. Notice the man has medium dark skin and irises and strong brows and mustache. What is prominent, however, is the intense whites of his eyes. This would make him high contrast and have the ability to wear black and white.

When we take a picture with a camera, we want the picture to be in focus so that all the elements can be clearly seen. Wearing the appropriate level of contrast in an outfit creates a clear picture of you.

- Low contrast people have light hair, skin and eyes. They tend to look better in more blended color combinations with more closely related colors.

- Medium contrast individuals have medium color hair, medium skin tone, and medium color eyes, and can wear colors that are related in a medium way, i.e., dark brown with camel.

- High contrast people have strong coloring, i.e. dark hair, dark eyes, and light skin, or deep skin, dark hair, and contrasting teeth and whites of the eyes and can easily wear black and white.

The appropriate level of contrast in an outfit creates a clear picture of you.

DETERMINE YOUR LEVEL OF CONTRAST

This is the range in contrast you can wear in your clothing and look harmonious. When you wear your native level of contrast, you make yourself fully visible for someone else. When you wear too strong a contrast for your coloring, it overpowers you. Too low a contrast makes you disappear.

Hair Color

❑ Light - Blonde, Champagne, Mushroom
❑ Medium - Pecan, Amber, Strawberry blonde
❑ High - Auburn, Mahogany, Black

Skin Color

❑ Light - Alabaster, Cameo, Porcelain
❑ Medium - Tawny Peach, Light Bronze, Light Olive, Cafe Latte
❑ High - Red Bronze, Rose Copper, Indian Red, Deep Olive

Eyes

❑ Light - Baby Blue, Light Hazel, Light Bronze, Seafoam Green
❑ Medium - Blue, Nutmeg, Maple, Pine Needle Green, Hazel
❑ High - Cinammon, Copper Brown, Onyx, Black-Brown, Walnut

Hair to Skin

Low Contrast   Medium Contrast   High Contrast

Eyes to Skin

Low Contrast   Medium Contrast   High Contrast

Eyes to Hair

Low Contrast   Medium Contrast   High Contrast

What is your overall range based on the three levels of contrast?

Low Contrast   Medium Contrast   High Contrast

Example of Low Contrast
Kim's hair, skin, and eyes are of equal value representing
a light tonal quality.

Example of High Contrast
Christine has dark copper brown eyes and darker hair
contrasting with light skin.

It's important to recognize your range; not a specific category.

TWO

TEXTURE

THE PRINCIPLE OF TEXTURE

TEXTURE

**Creates Interest and Harmony:
By choosing clothing and
accessories that repeat the
texture of your hair and skin,
you create a look that is
dynamic and harmonious.
The more variation in your
facial features, the more
texture you should wear.**

This is a very exciting principle since it allows us to begin reflecting ourselves through our choices in fabrics and accessories. Correctly reflecting our texture presents a harmonious vision to the viewer. Texture specifically refers to the gradations of color and surface interest present in our hair, skin, and eyes. I'm going to first talk about it in terms of Mother Nature. As I said before she's the author of design in our life. So I'd like you to go outside into a garden or some favorite place, and look at all the textures.

You can see the different gradations of texture in the leaves of a tree. Groupings of flowers present varying textures and design as they are interwoven together. If you look at the bark of the tree or stems on flowers, the texture of the earth, soil, rocks, and sand – all of that creates surface design. Remember, the design pattern that we work with is all about repeating the design pattern already created in you. Somehow, we become conditioned into believing that our unique design pattern is somehow flawed, and the grass would be greener if only…(you can fill in the blank).

In other words, if you have straight hair, you wish it was curly. If you have curly hair, you wish it was straight. If you have freckles, you wish it was peaches and cream, if you have wrinkles, you wish your skin was smooth. I'm here to tell you that your design pattern is something to be celebrated and I want to offer an alternate way of thinking. I see all these areas as points of interest. If we were having a conversation and there was no punctuation, you would eventually fall asleep because my voice would offer no dynamic or interest to keep you engaged. The same is true for people looking at you. Your points of interest, which show up as your unique design patterns, engage the viewer's eye and make you interesting. When you offer repetition of your native design in the texture of the clothing and accessories you wear, you wake up the viewer's eye and keep it dancing. The movement is kept alive through your varying points of interest. If the eye is only looking at the face it's limited in its range of motion.

Now, we are going to take a personal inventory so you can begin to discern your points of interest. Turn to the workbook pages at the end of this chapter. Let's begin with smooth texture. Is your hair smooth, wavy, or is it curly? If your hair is smooth then place a check mark in the smooth column. If it's medium, which means sort of wavy, then place a check mark in the medium texture column, and if it's curly, then place a check mark in the rugged texture column. The next thing I look at is how many shades of color does your hair have? Is your hair one value? Is it solid brown or solid black? If yes, then place a check mark in the smooth texture column. Does it have a couple of shades? Do you have a couple of highlights? If yes, then place a check mark in the medium texture column. If your hair has many shades, then you would place a check mark in the rugged texture column.

The next thing we look at are your facial features. The first thing to observe is whether your facial features (your eyes, eyebrows, nose, and mouth) are consistent in size. If you look at your eyes, eyebrows, nose, and mouth do they seem about the same size? If so check the smooth column. How many of these features are different in size? Are your eyes, eyebrows, and nose medium in size and you have a large mouth? Or do you have a medium size mouth, large eyes and eyebrows, and a small nose? Then you would check the medium texture column. If you have lots of size variation, for example you have small eyes, large eyebrows, medium nose, and a small mouth, then you would place a check mark in the rugged texture box. The more variation, the more texture is created.

The next thing we're going to look at is your skin, and this is interesting because I want to refer again to the bark of the tree. When we look at the bark of a tree, one of the things we find interesting in the bark is how many lines are in it, the various textures – some bark is really smooth and some have many variations. Let's look at your skin. Does your skin appear to have one tone in its coloring or pigmentation? If so, place a check mark in the smooth column. In the medium range, you might have basically one tone with perhaps a bit of rose in the cheeks. If you have lots of freckles, or freckles over the bridge of the nose, or lots of color variation, you would place a check mark in the rugged column. The other thing I want to add here is some people have what we call faceted features, and that also creates texture. Faceted features look like your face is divided into little pie shapes. You have little points at the end of your eyes and at the corners of your mouth. You might have a little pointed chin and prominent cheekbones. Katherine Hepburn has faceted features. Faceted features create rugged texture.

Finally, let's look at animation. Animation has to do with how much motion is in your face. Some people have very little expression in their face when they talk. Their face looks like a still life portrait with little or no movement of the facial muscles. That is what we call still and more static features. If so, you would place a check mark in the smooth column. Medium texture means that there is some movement in the facial muscles when you talk. For example, the eyebrows move when you talk, one eye becomes smaller than the other when you smile, your mouth crooks in one direction or the other when you talk. You could even see this in your eyes not being the same size or your nose flaring a bit when you speak. If so, you can place a check mark in the medium texture column. For the rugged column we look for lots of movement. If you usually talk with your hands, you talk with your face. There's some kind of motion that's happening. You smile a lot, raise your eyebrows, have big dimples, your skin crinkles around the eye area when you speak, and so on. That's what we call animated.

Now tally up your columns. You might have two in the medium texture and three in the rugged or you might have one in the smooth, two in the medium, and the rest in the rugged, giving you a scale of medium to rugged texture for your clothing. The idea is to see that given this kind of inventory, the people who can wear smooth texture, have the smooth hair, hair that's one color, features that are consistent in size, skin that appears smooth and of one shade, and features that are more static. The type of texture you would wear would be found in a gabardine suit or in satin finish. Anything that usually has some metallic and shine to it also creates a sense of smoothness. You could also wear a silky knit like rayon or velvety texture like velour.

People who wear medium texture might have wavy hair, a couple of tones in the shades of their hair, features with a slight variation in size, a little bit of animation in the face, and just a little bit of pigment variation to the skin. An example of medium texture would be a pique knit or a medium weight corduroy, ribbing in a sweater or T-shirt, embroidery or lace. Suede is also a good example of medium texture. Now let's review the rugged texture. This is someone with naturally curly hair with many shades, with lots of variation in the size of their features, their skin could be freckled, wrinkled or ruddy and the facial features have lots of movement and animation. Examples of rugged texture is mohair, herringbone, heavy corduroy, cable knit sweaters, and boucle or chenille.

After you've done the inventory, go into your closet and select the top five outfits that you wear and see how much texture is in the clothing. Is there a relationship between your favorite items and your texture? Remember in this work the idea is to recreate the design pattern that you have, exactly the way it is without changing anything. Practice holding up clothing that matches your level of texture and see how you like it. If the appropriate texture is not in your closet of accessories, you can create a shopping list of new additions that will spice up your wardrobe.

..your unique design patterns engage the viewer's eye
and make you interesting.

SMOOTH TEXTURE creates simple design

1

2

3

1 Notice her smooth straight hair and smooth skin that is all one tone.

2 Notice the tall smooth columns with the soft ribbing and wide spacing in between.

3 Notice the calm smooth water.

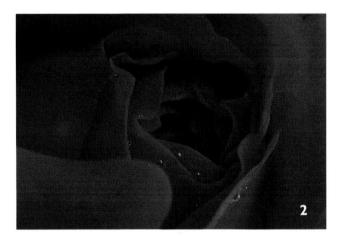

1 She has soft wavy curls, slight pigment variation and her features are similar in size.

2 Notice the curves of the flower match the outer curve of her face. The center of the flower matches the curl of her hair.

3 The rounded line and color creates a lightness and playfulness also found in her dimples and hair.

RUGGED TEXTURE

creates all over surface pattern and keeps the eye moving

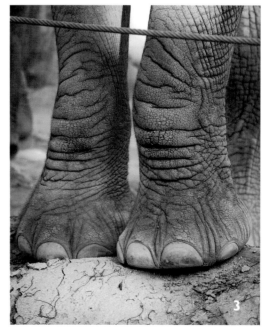

1 Textured skin and hands and pigment variation create texture.

2 The all over grooves and knotches create surface interest.

3 Deep wrinkles and lines create surface pattern.

IDENTIFY YOUR TEXTURE

Smooth Texture	Medium Texture	Rugged Texture

Smooth Texture

❏ Smooth hair

❏ Hair one color

❏ Facial features consistent in size (eyes, nose, mouth)

❏ Skin is smooth, one color

❏ Features appear still and static

Medium Texture

❏ Wavy hair

❏ Hair with slight toning

❏ Facial features have some variation in size

❏ Skin has some pigment variation

❏ Features have some movement

Rugged Texture

❏ Curly hair

❏ Hair has many shades

❏ Variation in size of facial features

❏ Skin has ruddiness, freckles, many colors

❏ Features are animated

Texture equals the amount of surface interest in a fabric. The greater the surface interest, the greater the texture. Listed here is an inventory of what creates various forms of surface interest and texture for you.

Based on your answers, what type of surface interest should your fabrics have:

Smooth Texture   Medium Texture   Rugged Texture

←———→

Smooth Texture creates simple design. Wear smooth texture with solids.

Medium Texture is not too busy and not plain. Wear simple textures like pique, linen.

Rugged Texture creates all over surface pattern and keeps the eye moving. Wear mohair, boucle, chenille and raw silk.

THE PRINCIPLE OF TEXTURE

Amy has smooth hair, porcelain skin, and some animation in her facial features. The texture in her outfit is smooth except for the scarf which has low to medium texture.

Anu has hair of many shades and textures, freckled skin and very animated features. Her clothes have lots of movement, texture, and design. She is medium to rugged texture.

Sunlight (Spring)

The warm glow of sunlight radiates new energy as
Mother Nature comes alive.

THREE

COMPLEXITY

THE PRINCIPLE OF COMPLEXITY

COMPLEXITY

Balance and Integrity:
The design of the hair, skin and eyes is repeated in the print, texture, and design throughout the body.
The more energy a person radiates the more complexity should be reflected.

Complexity is closely related to texture in that it is the amount of design that you can wear. Unlike texture, complexity takes your personal energy into consideration. The reason this is so important is that it creates the external or visual integrity between your inner and outer self. Let's first look at complexity in Mother Nature to make it easy for us. Walk to your favorite place, it may be a garden or outside in the park. Notice the tones in the green grass. You may be looking at the grass and see a brook or a meadow, some rocks or formation of rocks. We can see in the distance the different layers of the trees, the landscape, and the hills. All of that is creating complexity.

The complexity of design that Mother Nature gives us is a very important part of her gift to us and I'd like to review how we would experience it. Let's pretend we're meeting a friend for lunch and your friend appears in the doorway and you notice that she looks really beautiful. She's dressed in a print and has on several pieces of jewelry and earrings and a couple of necklaces and bracelets. You might even comment to yourself, "wow, she looks fantastic but I could never wear all of those accessories myself."

What this principle will teach you is the amount of design that you can wear to look congruent and interesting, but not overwhelmed by too much bulk. Some people like to wear lots of design and you may know someone like this, it may be you. They like to wear several necklaces, bracelets, earrings, belts, scarves and print designs. Other people say, "You know, I just don't like a lot of jewelry and I'd prefer to wear solids." The range of complexity again is the amount of busyness and detail that someone can handle in an outfit.

Something I pointed out earlier is that one of the most important factors in figuring complexity is your personal energy. Some people consider themselves to be sort of very quiet, introverted people. Some people are extroverted. They are the life of the party – when they walk in, the activity and life begins. And others feel a little bit of both. In terms of communication, you can use dress to language and promote yourself. Your clothes become the marketing tool that announces who you are and what you are about.

If you appear on the outside incongruent with your personal energy, you set up an expectation for those looking at you that can only lead to disappointment. We call that making the wrong first impression. Wouldn't it be awful to be dismissed by someone simply because the real you didn't show up? For example, you are this strong, independent, capable, highly energetic person and you show up dressed the opposite, in pastels or muted colors – the people who are attracted to that softer quieter energy are going to be surprised by what actually shows up when you begin talking. If someone is looking for that higher level of energy, you might get dismissed by your looks alone because an assumption was made that you were too quiet for what they were looking for. In my observation, people do this "opposite dressing" all the time because strong people want to minimize their strength so they dress too softly, people who are more reserved tend to dress stronger than their real persona out of self protection. What I am saying to you is that your strength, power, presence, and affinity lies in telling the truth about who you are for the world to see. One of the important things when you dress is being a gift not only to yourself, but to the rest of the universe in your clarity. The people and friends that you will attract will be people that you relate to on a much more intimate level because the connection is authentic. You don't have to redefine yourself to match up with the clothes you are wearing, the clothes are matching up with you.

When my clients first come to me, so many of them see their clothes as part of a uniform – something they put on to project a certain persona, like the power suit. I would offer that when your clothing is an extension of your inner self, you always appear powerful, authentic, and radiant.

Now, let's go through the list of what creates complexity. We're going to add four categories to the ones we completed when we reviewed texture. The four categories will be based on your energy: how fast you walk, the volume of your voice, how animated you are when you talk, and how you respond in conversation. Your energy plus your results for texture will determine your level of design. Can you wear simple design, medium design or complex design? First, let's talk about the way you walk. Do you have a slow, methodical, languid walk? If so, then check the simple category. Do you walk with a sense of purpose with a medium pace? If so, then check the medium category. Or are you someone who can be heard coming down the hall with lots of energy? You would check the complex category. Now let's look at how you talk. Do you have a soft, quiet voice and speak at a slow pace? Then check the simple column. Do you have a medium range and pitch to your voice and speak at a medium pace? If so, check the medium design column. Or are you very animated with lots of tonality and range to the way you speak and we can hear you talking down the hall even when you whisper? Check the complex column.

Now let's talk about animation. Do you use your hands when you speak or are you more still or maybe not even gesture at all? If you are more still with your body when you talk check the simple design column. Do you have a slight movement of your head and possibly gesture with your hands, once in a while just to emphasize your point? Then check the medium design column. People who need the most complexity have lots of movement when they speak. The body is moving, the head is moving, they're smiling a lot, they're frowning a lot, they're moving their body and they're moving their hands.

Finally, let's take a look at conversation. When someone asks you a question, do you answer yes or no and typically not offer up more information unless you are asked? If this is you, check the simple design column. When someone asks you a question, do

One of the most important factors in
figuring complexity is your personal energy.

you often simplify your answers to short sentences or add humor to your response? If so, check the medium column. And finally, when you are asked a question, do you like to respond with lots of detail or tell a story? If so, check the complex column.

Take a look at your answers. Don't worry about definites – what we're really looking for is your range. Are you low to medium complexity, are you medium to high complexity? If your answers were simple design, then dressing in solid colors is best for you. You might accessorize with a pair of earrings and a necklace but not also with bracelets. You might wear only bracelets with no necklace or you might wear a ring and earrings. Minimal design is best for you.

Then we have medium design. Those are people who might wear a print scarf once in awhile. You might have a couple of print skirts or shirts in your wardrobe that you would pair up with a solid. I like some patterning on shirts as long as it's not too busy. You would accessorize with earrings and a necklace. You could wear a couple of bangles. You might add a belt to your outfit.

The complex person would wear an all-over print or print on print. You can wear earrings, with multiple necklaces of different lengths and textures, many bracelets and rings. You can not only wear patterned clothing but lots of texture as well. The idea is when you repeat the design pattern in your face, your facial features, the design of your hair and the way your body moves, you create a sense of integrity and harmony and balance that invites people, like a beautifully wrapped gift, to find out who you are and what you are up to.

LOW COMPLEXITY Stillness and spaciousness in design is important

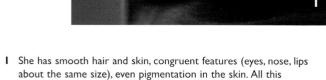

1 She has smooth hair and skin, congruent features (eyes, nose, lips about the same size), even pigmentation in the skin. All this creates   simplicity in design.

2 One can interpret a rapturous moment captured in time. The smooth marble, simplicity in the curves, and soft quality of the moment creates simplicity in design.

3 Notice a subtlety in the radiance and the nuance of shadows that create a sense of stillness.

1 Medium definition in the flowers, leaves, and sky lend to medium complexity.

2 Her wavy hair, animated face, and smooth complexion equates with a medium amount of design.

3 The grass and stepping stones create space while the flowers, trees, and shrubs create design. The combination is medium complexity.

HIGH COMPLEXITY Movement with texture on texture

1 Notice her curly textured hair, variation in size of her features, and animated, energetic personality. This combination allows her to wear a maximum amount of design.

2 The ribbing in the shells, color variation, and textured rope creates a busyness.

3 Lots of texture in the trees and in the leaves on the ground creates lots of movement, texture, and design.

4 The abundant texture, variation in size, and variation in color tones create lots of design.

YOUR LEVEL OF COMPLEXITY

Complexity is defined as the amount of design, texture and movement that a person can wear in an outfit. This would include print versus solid, texture versus smooth, or lots of accessories versus simple adornment.

Listed below are the factors that create simple design versus complex design. This design factor applies to interiors as well as clothing design selection.

Simple Design	Medium Design	Complex Design
❑ Slow, methodical walk	❑ Walk with some animation	❑ Energetic walk with lots of movement
❑ Speaks slowly, quietly	❑ Speaks with some modulation	❑ Speaks quickly, loudly
❑ Little animation when speaking	❑ Uses some gestures when speaking	❑ Lots of gestures when speaking
❑ Black and white answers	❑ Likes a small amount of discussion	❑ Many details in answers

Some people can wear lots of design – several necklaces, bracelets, earrings, belts, scarves and print design. Others wear very little jewelry and solids. The range of complexity is the amount of busyness and detail that someone can handle in an outfit.

What is your range of complexity? _____

Low Complexity   Medium Complexity   High Complexity

⟵————————————————————————————⟶

THE PRINCIPLE OF COMPLEXITY

Katherine has a stronger energy, a very intentional walk, and speaks in a voice with more volume. She reflects medium to high complexity as seen in the many layers of her clothing, different textures, and the amount of jewelry and accessories.

Annie has buoyant energy, a liveliness to her walk, and speaks more softly. She is low to medium complexity. Her clothes reflect this complexity as seen in the scarf, texture in the belt, and combination of colors.

Twilight (Summer)

Mother Nature sustains her energy appreciating one
gentle moment flowing into the next.

FOUR

Scale & Proportion

THE PRINCIPLE OF SCALE AND PROPORTION

SCALE & PROPORTION

Creates balance and symmetry: When you wear the appropriate size accessories (eyewear, necklace, earrings, tie, scarf, belt), the body looks balanced and integrated.

So far we have discussed the level of contrast you can wear and the level of texture and complexity in your fabrics, prints, and accessories. The next principle is scale and proportion and has to do with the size and shape of print designs and accessories. It could be the size of the jewelry for a woman, the size of the print in a tie for a man, the detail in a pair of shoes or handbag. Proper scale and proportion gives the body a sense of appropriate balance. The best visual I can give to describe this would be to think about a sunflower. It has a long thick stalk with hearty leaves and, of course, the sunflower is a large burst of yellow and brown. It's in perfect proportion for its size. If we were to take a pansy and put it on top of the sunflower stalk with its large leaves, it would not only look incongruent and completely out of balance but would practically disappear from being overwhelmed. This same principle holds true for a tree. Imagine the trunk of a tree and the size of the branches – could you see too small a trunk with branches too large? The tree would tip over. Many people everyday make choices that have them looking like that unbalanced sunflower or tree. Balance is very important to the viewer because when we appear in balance, we appear in harmony and grounded. This is very important when trying to negotiate an idea with someone or in building trust and rapport with others quickly.

In determining the correct scale and proportion for you, you need to consider two things: the size of your face in proportion to your height and second, the sizes of your facial features in relation to your face. You could actually have a small face for your height, like myself. You could have a medium size face for your height, like Vanessa Williams, or you could have a large face in proportion to your height, like Nancy Reagan. To be accurate in this determination, you'll need to stand in front of a full length mirror – you might ask a friend how they see your proportions. Write down your answer. Now, let's look at the size of your features in proportion to the size of your face. Look at your largest feature first, which may be your eyes, your nose, or your mouth,

When we appear in balance, we appear in harmony and grounded.

and then compare the rest of your features including your eyebrows. Are they larger or smaller than the other? Write this down. Your sizes may be all around the same or they may vary. You may have large eyebrows, small eyes, medium nose, and a large mouth. Now look in a full length mirror at the overall size of your facial features.

Another way to evaluate this, if you are having some difficulty, is looking at whether your features are compact and close together or if there is a big distance between your eyebrows and mouth. Typically, if you measure the space between the middle of your eyebrows to the corner of your mouth, the space is 3 inches or 5 inches. Three inches usually indicates compact features and therefore smaller prints and smaller sized accessories. As you can guess by now, all the principles are around the idea of repetition. Small head and small features equal small print and accessories, medium head and medium features equal medium prints and accessories and large head and large features equal large prints and accessories. If you have a head to body proportion that is different than the proportion of your facial features, like a large head with small features, you would then wear a large print but with small details in it, like a large paisley pattern or large jewelry with small details around or on it. If you have a small head but large features you would wear both small and large prints and accessories. By this I mean, your necklace could have small or medium-sized beads, your print could have small or medium scale in the design or you might wear a larger accessory with a smaller print in the design of your shirt. It's all about setting a rhythm in repetition.

Many of my clients thought that their height dictated the size of their prints and accessories, so my petite clients would wear itty bitty jewelry and no prints, looking out of proportion because they, in fact, had larger features and needed that repetition in their design. How of many of you thought that shorter people would look even shorter if they wore larger patterns and accessories? As you can see, height is only part of the answer.

Let's say you want to buy a beautiful set of jewelry including earrings, necklace, and bracelet, and you have medium features with medium scale. Then you are going to go buy a medium size earring and necklace with medium detail. The detail could be in the ribbing, it could be in the texture of the earring, it could be a hammered earring for example, it could be a leaf size that is medium in range, it could be a round circle.

Standing in front of a full length mirror, hold it up to your eyes and your face. Ask yourself whether the size of the jewelry is getting lost and you can hardly see it or if it's so big that you are staring at it, not seeing you. I used to fall in love with a piece of jewelry and never really looked at myself wearing it – rather, I'd stare at the jewelry and love the color or the style and that's all I took into consideration. Prints get busy when they are too small for the size of your facial features and head. What's important is to understand the range because your proportions may vary from being one size to various sizes. The thing to think about is should you be wearing small, small to medium, medium, medium to large or large. Once you know this, you have the rule for buying watches, for selecting the details on a scarf or a pair of shoes, for selecting the print in your dress or the size of beads or stones on your earrings or necklace.

What happens in communication when we are wearing too big or too small accessories and prints, is that the viewer is drawn away from the message you are trying to give and drawn to the accessories or the busyness of the prints. Whereas if the accessories work and are in proportion – we look back at you, and notice, indeed the accessories are an enhancement to you.

Proper scale and proportion gives the body a sense of appropriate balance.

1 She has a larger head for her height with medium small features allowing her to wear some larger design as long as it has small to medium detail.

2 Her medium to small features determine the size and design in her necklace.

3 The round bowls reflect the curve of her features and round cheeks with small inner design in the bowls to pick up her features. As you can see, these design principles can be applied to every object, flower, clothing, jewelry, furniture and even cars.

4 The roundness of the flowers pick up the shape of her face with the smaller detail inside the bloom which mirrors the detail of her medium small features.

5 The binding, frog closures, and print design mirror the refinement and size of her facial features.

MEDIUM SCALE & PROPORTION

1   She has a medium size face for her height with medium small features and her hair is wavy with texture.

2   The animal print is medium in size and the spacing duplicates the spacing of her features, i.e. hairline to brow, brow to mouth, and mouth to chin.

3   The larger shapes in the tapestry mirrors the overall size of her face. The intricate detail recreates her features and hair texture. The blended quality of the print allows the woman to wear a larger amount of design that might otherwise be overwhelming.

4   She has small faceted features with points around her mouth and eyes and nose. These points are reflected in the sections of the large flower depicted in the center of the scroll. The overall design has lots of movement and equates with the dynamic of her energy (see Workbook on complexity).

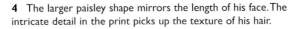

1 He has dramatic features that are larger in scale for his face.

2 The shirt collar shape mirrors the angle of the man's jaw line and the size of the collar balances his larger features.

3 The distance between the undulating curves duplicates the spacing of his features, i.e. hairline to brow, brow to mouth, and mouth to chin.

4 The larger paisley shape mirrors the length of his face. The intricate detail in the print picks up the texture of his hair.

Your Scale and Proportion

Scale and proportion are crucial in determining the appropriate size of accessories, prints, clothing and interiors. Our general understanding of these elements is only part of the story. We seem to think that tall people wear large accessories and short individuals wear small accessories.

The following inventory will help you determine your scale and proportion and the size of accessories to wear.

Scale and proportion is first defined by the size of your face in relation to your height and the proportion of your features on your face.

❑ Small in height (5'2") with a large head and large features, you wear large accessories.

❑ Medium in height (5'4" to 5'6") with a medium head and medium features, you wear medium accessories.

❑ Medium to tall in height (5'7" and up) with small features, you wear small accessories.

What is your height?
Small   Medium   Tall

What size is your head in proportion to your body?
Small   Medium   Large

What size are your features?
Small   Medium   Large

Do you have a compact face?

Based on these observations, what size accessories should you wear?
Small   Medium   Large

Notice the size of my head in proportion to my body and my compact features. The size of my features are picked up in the details and texture of the shirt and jacket. The size of the collar, pin, and buttons are in scale with my features. The deep V of the neckline creates the illusion of length balancing the proportion of my head to my body.

First notice the shape of my jaw. The square shape is repeated in the quilting pattern of the jacket. Without the smaller squares, the jacket would be overpowering instead of dramatic.

FIVE

GEOMETRY

PRINCIPLE OF GEOMETRY

GEOMETRY

Congruency and Repetition:
When you repeat, not compete,
with the geometric shapes
found in your body, you express
the fascinating design pattern
that you were born with.

This principle is meant to teach you how to evaluate yourself in terms of shapes. When I look at someone's features, what I see are shapes, literally, I mean like triangles, ovals, teardrops, and rectangles. That's why I don't make judgements around beauty. I'm always just looking for the balance and harmony in someone, the same way I evaluate the balance and harmony in a great work of art. Remember, what I keep saying is that the key to establishing balance and harmony lies in repetition. In order for you to begin this exercise, you need to understand what your shapes are. There are two things to look at: the outer shape of your face and the shape of your features. Once you understand this, you will know what shapes work for you in your prints, jewelry, necklines, belt buckles, shoe shapes, handbags, etc. You want to determine your body's geometry and repeat it in how you dress.

We're going to begin by first tying back your hair and getting in front of a mirror. Sometimes this is easier to do with a friend. Take a look at the shape of your face, using your hairline as your guide. The idea is to look at the outer shape of the face and your jaw line. The most common face shapes are round, oval, square, rectangle, and triangle. The round face has a soft arch along the forehead and jaw line, and width in the cheekbone area. An oval, on the other hand, also has a soft arch on the forehead and jaw line but the face is more narrow and long. A square face shape has more width to the face with a broad, wide forehead and jaw line with pretty straight sides. A rectangular face has a broad straight forehead and jaw line with straight sides and like the oval face, the face is more narrow and long than it is wide. The inverted triangle or heart shape is defined as having a broad forehead with a tapered chin, where the taper begins at the earlobe and ends at the chin. After observing your face shape, get a piece of paper and draw it – you may use the workbook pages as your guide.

The angle of the jaw line determines the angle of the shirt collar or the shape of the neckline. Square jaw lines look best in square necklines or crew neck; oval jaw lines look best in oval necklines and triangle jaw lines look best in V-necks. I think you are getting where I'm going with this. Try some different necklines in the mirror and see how flattering it is when you repeat the shape of your jaw line.

Let's see what other shapes are present when we take a look at your facial features. When looking at your face, imagine carving a pumpkin at Halloween. We use shapes to represent the eyes, nose and mouth. Usually, triangles for the eyes and nose and jagged triangles or squares for the teeth. I want you to look at your facial features as representative of shapes like those on the pumpkin. Starting with the eyebrows, typical brow shapes could be a triangle, more round or arched, like the arch of a doorway, or like a wedge which is straight across with thickness.

Next, let's look at your eyes. Are they teardrop-shaped, which would be more pointed on the outside and rounder by the nose; almond-shaped which comes to a point at both ends; a half moon which is more straight on bottom and curved on top; or soft triangles where they are more straight towards the nose area and pointed at the ends? I also want you to consider your eye sockets. On some people the eye sockets are very round and prominent which would allow them to wear circular shapes.

Next, let's look at your nose. Is it angled like the beak of an eagle? We call this aquiline. Do you have a straight nose where the bridge and the end of your nose are in a straight line? The next shape is teardrop – narrow bridge, straight with a slight flare, comes to a soft point. Your nose could be more triangular if you are narrow at the top and wider along the bottom. You could have a button nose which is rounded at the top, and finally, piquant-shaped which is curved with the end of the nose turned up in a point.

Now let's examine your mouth. Is it straight, especially in the middle of the lip where your lips arch up into points; diamond-shaped where the points on the upper lips create a triangle where they meet? Is it arched where there is almost no point at all at the center, or do you have more of a pout where your mouth appears more round? Add all these observations to your drawing. The point of this exercise is to become familiar with the overall design of your face. Use it as a reference point when you buy prints, patterns, and accessories.

In repeating your native design pattern you create drama and interest.

After you've done this exercise, have a friend draw your face from their perspective. It's fun to compare the results. Now write down the list of shapes that are present in your face shape and facial features. You now know what shapes are most flattering for you in prints and accessories. You could have triangular-shaped eyes, a teardrop nose, arched eyebrows and an oval face. If you wanted to buy a pattern in a scarf or ties, you could look for a pattern of teardrops and triangles and ovals. In accessories, you could purchase oval or teardrop-shaped earrings, and an oval belt buckle. The shape of the toe of the shoe could be pointed like a triangle or oval, but not square.

I'd like you to take a look at one last important thing in understanding your geometry. This is the measurement of the length of your head. Measure your head from the top of your hair to the chin. Usually this measurement is 8 inches. Now measure from where your neck meets the shoulder to the center of your chest. This is the ideal length for a V-neck, necklace, knot of a scarf, or lapel. If it's too short, somehow you look cut off or crowded. If you wear too long of a neckline, it makes your head seem smaller and out of proportion. For those of you who have deep V-necks because of the length of your head, and wish to be more modest, consider wearing camisoles under your V-neck blouses, shirts, and cardigans. The camisole should be the same color as whatever you are wearing on the bottom.

In conclusion, the whole idea of this exercise is to familiarize yourself in terms of geometric shapes. In repeating your native design pattern you create drama and interest. If you are wearing design patterns that are in opposition to your native design pattern the viewer sees a lot of conflict and confusion rather than harmony.

The spacing of the print in her top reflects the spacing of her features. The placement of the print is triangular which repeats her jaw line. The width of the disc in her necklace mirrors the width of her face. The length of the necklace is directly proportional to the length of her head.

Diana has a triangular jaw line. Her jaw line is picked up in the lapels of her jacket and in the butterfly pin at her waist.

PRINCIPLE OF GEOMETRY

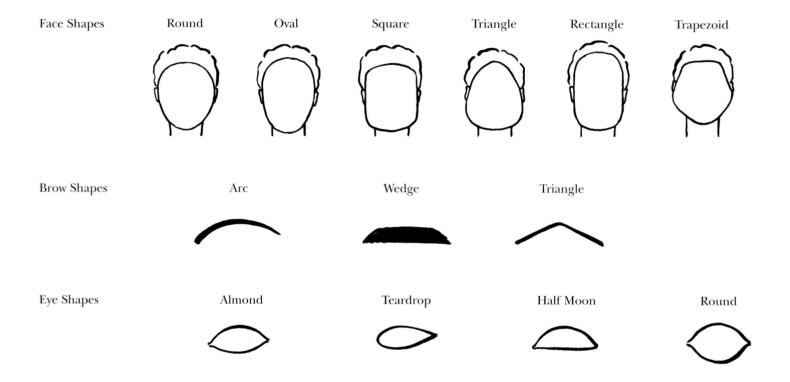

Face Shapes   Round   Oval   Square   Triangle   Rectangle   Trapezoid

Brow Shapes   Arc   Wedge   Triangle

Eye Shapes   Almond   Teardrop   Half Moon   Round

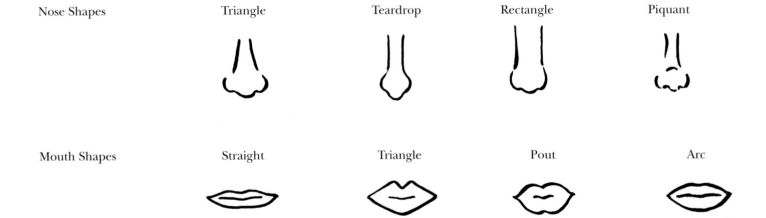

Nose Shapes   Triangle   Teardrop   Rectangle   Piquant

Mouth Shapes   Straight   Triangle   Pout   Arc

SIX

VISUAL WEIGHT

VISUAL WEIGHT

**Alignment and Flow:
When you align with your
body type and visual weight of
your hair, skin, and features,
you honor the natural flow of
your body.**

Next I want to talk about visual weight. Fabrics play an important role in how clothing drapes on your body. It's important to know what type of fabric is appropriate for you, as well as what type of fabric enhances your body structure. To determine this, stand in front of a mirror so that you can answer the following questions. First, what is the visual weight of your hair? Is your hair very fine or very thick or somewhere in between? Fine hair would give you a lighter weight fabric; medium thickness, medium weight fabric; thick hair, heavy weight fabric. Now, let's look at your skin. The range is from very transparent skin to lots of freckles, wrinkles, or ruddiness. Indicate the corresponding answer with light weight, medium weight, or heavy weight fabric.

Finally, let's look at your features. Do you have really strong eyebrows and prominent features? Are your features around medium in size and weight? Or do you have really delicate, refined features? Again, you could experience a range with heavy weight hair, medium weight features, and light weight skin. The visual weight of the fabric is based around that. You might have a heavy weight jacket, a medium weight skirt and light weight accessories. The idea is to balance that visual weight in every single outfit that you wear. For the man it could be a heavy weight tweed jacket, medium slacks and a light weight shirt and a medium print tie. The key again lies in the repetition.

One of the things I discovered after working with over 5,000 clients is that the weight of the fabric corresponds with your nature. Light weight fabrics are really important to people with fine, transparent skin. Flowing light weight fabrics feel good to your body. If you have a more substantial body and strong features and heavy weight hair, to wear something lightweight seems inconsequential. Likewise, when you wear something too heavy, it looks burdensome. It doesn't equate with the strength of your physicalness.

When you dress according to your visual weight
you honor the natural flow of your body.

Let's review one more element in this area before I give you a list of fabrics that work for you. I work with three different body types – skeletal, muscular and molded. The flow of fabrics needs to flow with the structure of the body. Usually there is variation of three body types:

Skeletal is someone who has a wiry, taut frame and is more boney in their body structure. They need textured fabrics and fabrics that have body, structure, and thickness. This could be a heavily starched shirt that has a pattern or some texture, a leather jacket that has some body to it or a more structured jacket, or a pencil skirt that has some stiffness to it. I think of the fabric as filling out the skeletal body.

Next is the **muscular frame** – I equate athletic with muscular. The athletic body needs a semi-structured shoulder and fluid body drape. We are looking at fabrics that move with the body and at the same time retain their shape. You could find this in stretch jeans, stretch gabardine, knits and jersey-like fabrics, like a T-shirt dress or a suit by St. John.

The **molded body** is like the rubenesque paintings. A rubenesque body is full of curves. They have a fuller bust, tummy and derriere and need fluid fabrics with softness and drape. This body type looks best in a soft suit, a sweater dress, cardigans or shirts without collars.

Fabrics that work well with the skeletal frame are fabrics that have body: suede, gabardine, leather, raw silk, Thai silk, tapestry, pique, corduroy, velvet, broadcloth, chambray, cotton lace, organdy, faille, mohair, grosgrain, taffeta, embroidered and encrusted lace, flannel, tweeds, linen, and heavier knits.

Fabrics that work well with the muscular frame are fabrics that are not bulky or too thick: light to medium weight knits, soft suede and chamois, silk noile, silk knits, silk shantung, light weight linen, fine corduroy, wool and rayon challis, wool crepe, panne velvet, velour, silk damask, chenille, silk lame, soft brocade, tweeds, and boucle knits.

Fabrics that work well with the molded body are fabrics that are fluid with drape: cotton and rayon jersey, light weight cashmere, crepe de chine, chiffon and georgette, gauze, lawn, batiste, voile, wool voile, soft knits, sheer crochet, delicate lace, mohair, sheer wool, wool and rayon challis.

The weight of the fabric corresponds with your nature.

1 The fish are light in color and the fins are transparent.

2 Her hair is light in color and fine in texture. Her skin is one tone and has a translucent quality.

3 The flower is sheer and buoyant in nature with light weight points.

MEDIUM VISUAL WEIGHT

1 Her brown hair is medium in weight as are her features
   and green eyes.

2 The medium shade of green and the visual weight of the foliage
   creates medium weight.

3 The green grapes, although light in value, are opaque and the
   clusters are medium in density.

1 He is made of heavy stone with deep carving and high relief, creating the feeling of strength.

2 The sculptured hedges, trees, and rocks have density, substance, and weight. The close placement of the individual plants and rocks add to the visual weight.

3 She has dark thick hair, strong brows, and intense eyes which all add to her visual weight.

4 The shell has depth of shading, strong contours, and layers of texture.

YOUR VISUAL WEIGHT

Nikki has very thick hair, deep set eyes, a prominent nose and cheekbones. She can wear medium to rugged texture and medium to high complexity. Therefore, she can handle more visual weight.

Thick hair, pominent features and skin with pigment variation call for fabrics that are heavy weight, for example, a cable knit sweater and corduroy slacks.

Medium weight hair, skin and features call for medium weight fabrics.

Lightweight hair, transparent skin and delicate features require lightweight fabrics.

A combination of thick hair, medium features, and lightweight skin requires a mixture of weights worn together.

Determine your visual weight:

Hair:

Fine hair shaft	=	Lightweight fabrics
Medium hair shaft	=	Medium weight fabrics
Thick hair shaft	=	Heavy weight fabrics

Skin:

Transparent skin	=	Lightweight fabrics
Medium weight skin	=	Medium weight fabrics
Skin with pigment variations	=	Heavy weight fabrics

Features:

Refined features	=	Lightweight fabrics
Medium features	=	Medium weight fabrics
Predominant features	=	Heavy weight fabrics

For the Skeletal Body
Fabrics that have body, structure and definition.

Suede, gabardine, leather, raw silk, Thai silk, tapestry, pique, corduroy, velvet, broadcloth, chambray, cotton lace, organdy, faille, mohair, grosgrain, taffeta, embroidered and encrusted lace, flannel, tweeds, linen, and heavier knits.

FABRICS AND BODY TYPES

For the Muscular Body
Fabrics should have form and ease.

Light to medium weight knits, soft
suede and chamois, silk noile, silk knits,
silk shantung, light weight linen, fine
corduroy, wool and rayon challis, wool
crepe, panne velvet, velour, silk damask,
chenille, silk lame, soft brocade, tweeds,
and boucle knits.

For the Molded Body
Fabrics should have flow and movement.

Cotton and rayon jersey, light weight
cashmere, crepe de chine, chiffon and
georgette, gauze, lawn, batiste, voile,
wool voile, soft knits, sheer crochet,
delicate lace, mohair, sheer wool, wool
and rayon challis.

SEVEN

PRINT SELECTION

THE PRINCIPLE OF PRINT SELECTION

The last principle is print selection. Prints, to me, are the animation of our life. I find them inspiring. Can you imagine walking into a home where there were no print pillows, pictures, print upholstery or rugs, or flowers, or plants in the room? It wouldn't be very exciting. So most people, even when intimidated at the thought of buying a pattern or print will venture to have at least a picture or two, or some pillows, an afghan, and plants in their home. However, that same person will wear only solid colors, usually black, white and navy, and no accessories when it comes to getting dressed.

Prints are a very important part in highlighting that which makes you interesting. Prints are the exclamation point. Wearing a print makes you look like a fascinating person to be around. We sell ourselves short when we don't dress in a way that reflects how unique and interesting we really are. There are many factors that enter into buying a print. All the elements we have been discussing will be taken into consideration. Should you buy a large or small print? You already know the answer from the exercise in scale and proportion. How much busyness you can handle was addressed in complexity. In terms of the print selection, one important part is the spacing of the print. Let's begin by measuring the space from the very top of your forehead to the center of the eyebrow. Then measure the center of the eyebrow to the corner of your mouth and from the corner of the mouth to the chin. If you are buying a plaid shirt, those three spacings give you the three different spacings of the plaid or stripe. If you are buying a print and your features are closely spaced, you would want a print that is more closely spaced.

I want to give you an example combining the principles of complexity, scale and proportion, and print design. I have a small face for my height, my features are close together and small to medium in size. I also have a compact face. If I buy a print that is too large and spaced too far apart, the print totally overpowers me. I need something smaller and prints that are close together. Once you get the spacing of the print and the size of the print, you can feel more educated in picking something that really is expressive of you!

PRINT SELECTION

When you discover the size and character of print that is right for you, you can have fun choosing prints that express different sides of your personality (your heritage, your inner child, your humor, etc.).

1   The square design of the chair mirrors my jaw line. The design in the chair mirrors the texture of my hair. The smaller detail of the chair and ruffles mirrors the small to medium size of my facial features.

2   The medium small stones in the choker pick up the visual weight of my skin. The spacing of the print mirrors the spacing of my mouth to chin and the jagged edges of the embroidery mirrors the texture of my hair.

3   The medium and small stones are clustered together to form a larger design. My face is three inches from brow to mouth creating what we call compact features. The brooch mirrors the compactness of my features in the detail.

4   The design is a large print with small details, mirroring the size of my facial features. It's close together mirroring the compactness of my face, and it has movement in the pattern which picks up the texture of my hair. It is also a vivid and bold pattern which mirrors my dynamic energy.

5   The statues are medium in size with refined detail. These again mirror medium scale with fine detail. The movement is a reflection of my textured hair and dynamic energy.

1 She has a medium-sized face for her height with medium features. Her belt and necklaces are medium in size. The print skirt and fringe on the jacket mirrors the texture of her hair.

2 The spacing of the stripes and the detail in his whiskers and mouth creates visual weight, movement, and strength in energy. All this is reflected in the outfit the woman is wearing.

3 The statue is medium in size with medium texture to her headpiece, and medium gradation of color on her robe.

4 The size and shapes of the print replicate the size of her face and features. The texture and color of the print recreate the texture and color of her hair.

1 She is medium in height with larger face and features. The pendant and the print design in the coat are larger in scale. The intricate detail recreates the texture in her hair.

2 Notice the larger diamond shape of the leaves outlining the rounder shape of the tapestry. The larger design of the print mirrors the larger features of her face and her hair is mirrored in the detail of the leaves.

3 The larger eye design of the feathers recreate the shape of her face and features.

4 Notice the large size of the furniture and guild work and also the large pattern in the wall paper.

PRINT SELECTION

Prints are an important part of any wardrobe and can be found in the print of a scarf, blouse, skirt, or jacket. Part of our hesitation in selecting a print is that we don't know how to choose one. Many of the elements we have discussed so far go into choosing a print: level of contrast, size of print, type of print, and complexity of design.

One of the important features of a print is that it repeats the spacing found in the face: forehead to eyebrow, eyebrow to mouth, and mouth to chin.

Measure the space between your:
Forehead and eyebrow _____
Eyebrow to lip _____
Lip to chin _____

Compact features are usually found in a 3" to 5" spacing.
More widely spaced features are usually found in a 5 1/2" to 7" spacing.
The measurements are merely a guideline to help you interpret spacing in patterns, stripes and plaids that would be appropriate for you.

Print Selection

❑ Widely spaced features create a widely spaced print, plaid, or stripe.
❑ Medium spaced features create a medium spaced print, plaid or stripe.
❑ Closely placed features create a closely spaced print, plaid or stripe.

Prints highlight that which makes you interesting.
Prints are the exclamation point.

The print design repeats the curve of her face and the arch of her lips and brow. The satin brocade fabric repeats the shine of her hair. She has smaller features and a larger face, therefore, she can wear a larger print with smaller details. The necklace shows again the idea of a larger size pendant with smaller details in the pattern as do her earrings. The texture of the necklace is repeated in the print pattern.

REFLECTIONS

Whether we're aware of it or not, our closets tell the real story of who we think we are, may have been, want to be, and sometimes are.

Day after day, so many of us get dressed, look in the mirror and think, "Something is wrong." So, we go back into our closets and put on another blouse or a different pair of slacks. Still, something doesn't feel right. We go shopping, and ask our friends and sales people for help. They filter in who they think we are, mixed with the latest fashion trends, and choose an outfit "just for us". It may look great on the hanger, but how does it feel while you're wearing it?

Over the last 25 years, thousands of people from all walks of life have come to me on their quest to look great. They may need to make an impact at an important social event or maybe they're going through a major life transition. They might be graduating, or have an important job interview, and want to know how to look, and what to wear. You might think that at least the supermodels have it all figured out, but they don't. They tell me they've been well paid for dressing like someone else, and have been doing so throughout their entire careers.

The majority of my clients begin their session with a confession. They tell me that almost every day, they open up their closets and are baffled. They stand face to face with an assortment of things, and struggle to pick out something that speaks to them. Whether we're aware of it or not, our closets tell the real story of who we think we are, may have been, want to be, and sometimes are.

From infancy, we're trained to look outside ourselves to find out who we are within. We learned all kinds of strategies to gain love and approval. Many of these strategies involved looking and dressing a certain way. We often dressed from a need for acceptance. Years later, when our parents, teachers and pals have retreated into the past, we may discover that our original attitudes and behaviors still run our lives and define our perceptions. We find ourselves deeply imbedded in an identity that's not actually our own, but is tailored to fit an outdated set of beliefs.

Why isn't the beauty we so easily see in nature
something we recognize in ourselves?

Our culture dictates inaccessible standards of beauty and presentation. We've been brainwashed to believe we're incomplete as we are. Why are we so afraid to admit that we might be beautiful? We judge ourselves harshly, rarely acknowledging what we've been given to work with.

When we look into the patterns and colors of a seashell, a flower petal or a butterfly, we discover a perfection that awakens within us a sense of awe and deep knowing. It is radiant beauty overflowing. Why isn't the beauty we so easily see in nature something we recognize in ourselves? It's ironic that something as fundamental and natural as this requires such conscious tending, but it does. That's because we're subject to the powerful messages our culture sends, with its fickle definitions of who is beautiful and who is not. I believe that, as a culture, we have lost our connection to our own inherent truth and beauty, and must now rediscover these qualities.

Authentic, radiant beauty is a God-given quality, something usually considered inaccessible and indefinable. Authentic beauty comes from within, a light inside. And when we look for it on the outside, we often run into all kinds of illusions and imposters. "You were born into this world in physical form. You are alive, right here, right now, in this body!" Yes, that's the big headline. How can we expect to express our inner light and vitality when we spend most of our time looking outside ourselves for the answers? I've found that adorning the body with colors that relate directly to our core essence transforms the otherwise mundane experience of life on Earth into a fun and spiritual journey.

I invite you to believe that you are
a perfect creation just the way you are.

When we regard dressing merely as superficial adornment, we shut down the breadth of our ability to be alive and expressive. I believe that clothing is a tangible conduit for the intangible. Our clothing can be an extension of our skin and a mirror of our essence, but we must first be willing to look inside, and identify this essence.

I can't say enough about the importance of honoring inner and outer beauty in equal proportions. You may think that wearing a great red dress or shirt will get you noticed, but if that garment has no connection to what's inside, what's the point? We all want to live a meaningful life, but no matter how fully we express ourselves in other arenas, we usually stop short when it comes to dressing ourselves. It's simply because very few of us have the information or the tools to dress as our true selves, in full self-expression.

From the moment we are born, others dress us: pink for girls, blue for boys. We grow up inside of our parents' sense of style and color. When we become teenagers, we usually get to choose our own clothes, but succumb to peer pressure, and are slaves to every possible fad or fancy. As we grow up, we may develop a personal style, but often it's based on the latest fashions, and a desire to either stand out or fit in with the popular norm.

All day long, we inhabit garments. If they don't match the particular unique formulation of who we are in essence, color, texture and form, we are hidden. We become lost underneath layers of costume, fashion and old habits. We lose our vitality, and we may even lose touch with ourselves. Our bodies deserve the truth by wearing clothing and colors that express who we are. Our souls deserve to shine. And, so, what we wear needs to be an extension of what's inside, making its way outside. We are exquisitely, spectacularly and perfectly beautiful!

I hope I've given you an exciting and new way to see yourself. Each of us is a walking work of art. By having the language to evaluate your features in a new way, you can then begin to use the concept of repetition in your clothing choices. I know this may seem complicated at first but with practice, you will be able to make choices that are flattering and enhancing to your appearance.

For those of you interested in understanding this work at the next level, I invite you to visit my website at www.jenniferbutlercolor.com and come to a free Guest Event. Being fully expressed is not only in form but in color as well. Being fully integrated in color and design is a powerful communication tool. With the visual experience making up as much as 55% of the message, it's even more significant to be out in the world presenting a harmonious and congruent picture of ourselves.

By having the language to evaluate your features in a new way, you can then begin to use the concept of repetition in your clothing choices.

WINTER ESSENCE The moonlight reflects the crystalline quality of the ice and snow

1 The print does not honor the exotic nature of Indira's essence.

2 The powerful contrast of neutral black and white and crystal beading express her dramatic personality.

1   Although the charcoal and white are basics they don't give us the vitality represented in David's personality.

2   Robust, unpredictable, with dash and bravado, David is dressed to express his dynamic, radiant essence.

1   The print is too strong and distracting. It does not express the subtlety of her persona.

2   The delicacy of the lace reflects the refinement of Pamela's essence and the texture of the vest recreates the luxurious quality of her hair.

1   The basic white on Tony is draining and diminishes the warmth and strength of his personality.

2   His shade of red is earthy, rich, and dynamic, representing the depth of his nature.

ACKNOWLEDGEMENTS

Special appreciations to Diana and Sid Syvertson who are my treasured friends and the benefactors of this book.

My heartfelt gratitude to Anu Fergoda, my business partner and dear friend. From editing the copy to creating the captions, from coordinating the photo shoot to selecting the iStock pictures and the countless meetings with our publisher, you did it all! Your steadfast commitment brought this book to fruition and made my vision a reality. Your intelligence illuminates, your strength sources and your passion enlivens. Thank you for keeping me on track and in spirit with my true commitment. Your contribution is indelible.

I extend my thanks to my other staff members: Carol, Melanie and Shadee, who are my guiding light.

The idea of this book was initiated many years ago with my dear friends, Pamela Gien, author of *The Syringa Tree* and Sunya Currie, who is my fairy godmother.

Linda Gray, star of the TV show *Dallas*, has been my heroine in her commitment to authentic beauty, inside and out.

Growing up with five brothers as the only girl, I thank them all for the invitation to accept my natural beauty.

Thank you to my parents, Bill and Maxine, as well as my brothers and their families who provided me with the foundation for love and community.

I'd like to extend a special thanks and acknowledgement to Maria Rangel of Mariaphotography.com for her care and talent in being able to reveal the essence of each person that she photographed for this book. I'd also like to acknowledge istockphoto.com for creating a website where we could access such a large library of quality photos.

A special thanks to all my clients who keep this work alive as they dress each day in their essence. The following people volunteered to be photographed for this book: Our spring or sunlight essences are Janice Evans, Amy Siu, Joan Hill, Annie Hill, and David Hill. Our summer or twilight essences are Kimberly Rawlings, Tassos Pappas, Cami Elen, and Pamela McMillan. Our autumn or firelight essences are Tony Pethebridge, Diana Syvertson, Katherine Moffat, Anu Fergoda, and Jean Graham. Our winter or moonlight essences are Indira Pethebridge, Christine Kingston, Dunbar Gibson, and Nikki Kilgore. A special note, the clothes worn in these photographs were not wardrobed, but rather, are from each clients' own personal collection. This is how my clients dress each and every day.

Our vision boards were done by a talented group of artists at a retreat in Northern California. I'd like to thank them for their passion in creating works of art reflective of the seasonal essences. Those people are: Kimberly Rawlings, Nienke Sjaardema, Penny Dyer, and Anu Fergoda.

Thank you to Rev. Michael Beckwith, Rikki Byers Beckwith and the Agape community who taught me that the ability to see essence comes from a compassionate heart.

My women's groups through the years have been an invaluable support. Nicole Becker and the Women Empowered team as well as my goddess group from Agape – we all live and breathe the essence of this work together.

I wish to thank Crystal McCoppin and her husband, Patrick, from McMac Publications for maintaining the integrity of my work and to Hortensia Chu for bringing her artistry to the printed page.

None of this could have been done without Rosa Rubio who keeps my house in divine order and to Jamaica, my 16 year old cat, who keeps me honest even when no one else is around.

Moonlight (Winter)

The sky reflects moonlight energy. Mother Nature's silhouette against the vivid colors is luminous with the crystalline quality of ice and snow.